FIND YOUR INNER
UNICORN

FIND YOUR INNER
UNICORN

A JOURNAL CELEBRATING MAGICAL LIVING

OLIVER LUKE DELORIE

THUNDER BAY
P·R·E·S·S
San Diego, California

Thunder Bay Press
An imprint of Printers Row Publishing Group
9717 Pacific Heights Blvd, San Diego, CA 92121
www.thunderbaybooks.com • mail@thunderbaybooks.com

Printers Row Publishing Group is a division of Readerlink Distribution Services, LLC. Thunder Bay Press is a registered trademark of Readerlink Distribution Services, LLC.

Correspondence regarding the content of this book should be sent to Thunder Bay Press, Editorial Department, at the above address. Author, illustrator, and rights inquiries should be sent to Quarto Publishing plc.

Conceived, edited, and designed by Quarto Publishing plc,
6 Blundell Street, London, N7 9BH, UK.
QUAR.338364

Thunder Bay Press
Publisher: Peter Norton • Associate Publisher: Ana Parker
Acquisitions Editor: Kathryn Chipinka Dalby • Editor: Dan Mansfield

Quarto Publishing
Deputy Art Director: Martina Calvio
Art Director: Gemma Wilson
Designer: Karin Skånberg
Project Editor: Anna Galkina
Editorial Assistant: Charlene Fernandes
Publisher: Samantha Warrington

ISBN: 978-1-64517-521-6

Printed in Singapore

24 23 22 21 20 1 2 3 4 5

MIX
Paper from
responsible sources
FSC® C016973

CONTENTS

Introduction	6
Believe in yourself	8
Grow your own horn	10
Your source of energy	12
Get your beauty sleep	14
Wild and free	16
Let your hair down	18
Sweet dragon dreams	20
Feedback loops	22
Dreamtime	24
The colors of you	26
Play with your family	28
Frolic in the forest	30
Summon your stripes	32
Sprinkle sugar	34
Interdimensional travel	36
The golden rules	40
Magic is real	42
Speak from your heart	44
Aim for your north star	48
Pie in the sky	50
Follow your bliss	52
Harness your horsepower	54
Flow like water	56
Believe in yourself	58
Go outside	60
How to move mountains	62
The colors of the rainbow	64
Grow your brain	66
You have permission	74

Forgive the bullies	76
What would a unicorn do?	78
Your monkey mind	80
Mirror mirror	82
Things you can't be taught	84
So good it's true	88
You are beautiful	90
Treasure map	92
Sweet solitude	94
Away with anxiety	96
The gift of giving	98
Twist and shout	100
How to be sad	102
Horse & clown around	104
Act as if	106
Your supersonic ears	110
Keep calm and ride a unicorn	112
Use your imagination	114
Get back on the unicorn	116
Wish upon a star	118
Sing your song	120
Your superpower	122
Use your night vision	124
Your learning style	126
Far from home	128
Nature spirits	130
You can fly	132
Create your own language	134
The way you look at things	136
How to solve problems	138

From the horse's mouth	140
Take your time	142
Find your tribe	144
Artistic science	146
You-nique	148
Invincible invisibility	152
The legend of 10,000 hours	154
Your piece of pie	156
Face your fears	158
Pull your weight	160
The secret to happiness	162
Explore the universe	164
Under the sea	166
As simple as a sandwich	168
Hightail it	170
Tell the truth	172
Be kind	174
ESP	176
Be here now	180
Experimental adventures	182
I am 100% responsible	184
Speak up	188
Avalanche of appreciation	190
The six types of ESP and their definitions	192
Credits	192

INTRODUCTION

Ever since the fourth century BCE, when the first records of our favorite single-horned beasts appeared, unicorns have inspired us to dance and dream (and lose our minds when we see a double rainbow).

From Asia to Europe, from the Middle East to India, nearly every culture and civilization has acknowledged the mythos of the incomparable unicorn in literature, art, and religion, based both on accounts of real-life sightings and on fabulously fictitious fantasies creatively conjured by poets, philosophers, artists, and other aficionados of folklore.

The Greek physician Ctesias described a tale he heard from a traveler: "There are in India certain wild donkeys which are as large as horses, and larger. Their bodies are white, their heads dark red, and their eyes dark blue. They have a horn on the forehead which is about a foot and a half in length."

Unicorns were so universally admired that not only did Aristotle (one of the most influential intellectuals in history) love to discuss them, but at the height of the contrived hype, when horns were ten times more precious than gold, the pope purchased one for 90,000 scudi (the equivalent of about $20,000 today). And it didn't stop there. Luckily for India, when a unicorn reportedly bowed down at the feet of Genghis Khan, he took it as a sign from his departed father and chose not to conquer the continent.

Now thanks to the internet, unicorn sightings aren't so rare. Just as unicorns haven't always come in horsey shapes and sizes (*unicorn* literally means "one horn"), we've now got cute and cuddly kitticorns and caticorns to paw at our imaginations, not to mention majestic uniwolves to appease the more masculine-minded.

Mark it on your calendar: National Unicorn Day is April 9, so get your pretty little hooves on a Unicorn Questing License (you will find them on the Lake Superior State University website), a whopper of an honor recognized worldwide with no expiry date. Then you can get in on the action, no matter how old or young you think you are.

Let this book be your guide on your personal journey to explore and express yourself in as many imaginatively playful ways as possible, so that you too may find your inner unicorn, and thus make magic and miracles materialize in every moment.

BELIEVE IN YOURSELF

When people don't seem to believe in you, it's usually because they don't believe in themselves. Between you and me, they haven't found their inner unicorn. You can't blame them: fantastic fabled creatures like you are quite rare, and people often don't appreciate what they don't understand.

But just because they don't believe in what they can't see doesn't mean you have to doubt yourself and deny your genetic bucking-bronco blessings. You are a beautiful, gracious, and sophisticated-yet-playful creature who knows how to have fun. Know how you can help the haters? The easiest way to get them to believe in you is to believe in them.

I BELIEVE...

Write in colored pencils or pens every positive quality you believe to be true about yourself, and underneath describe the last time you proved they were real.

GROW YOUR OWN HORN

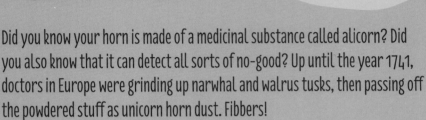

Did you know your horn is made of a medicinal substance called alicorn? Did you also know that it can detect all sorts of no-good? Up until the year 1741, doctors in Europe were grinding up narwhal and walrus tusks, then passing off the powdered stuff as unicorn horn dust. Fibbers!

If only they knew—like you do—how the imagination works. All you need to do is close your eyes, take a deep breath, and sprout the real thing out of your third eye. Now aim it up at the sky and spellbind lesser mortals into doing your bidding with your paranormal pony powers. No one stands a chance against your worldly wizardry.

Sculpt your own miniature—or life-sized—"uni-horn" out of modeling clay, cardboard, or construction paper. Decorate it with your favorite colors, shiny ribbon, and glitter, and proudly don it like a crown (or use it to empower a stuffed toy).

SCULPT YOUR OWN "UNI-HORN"

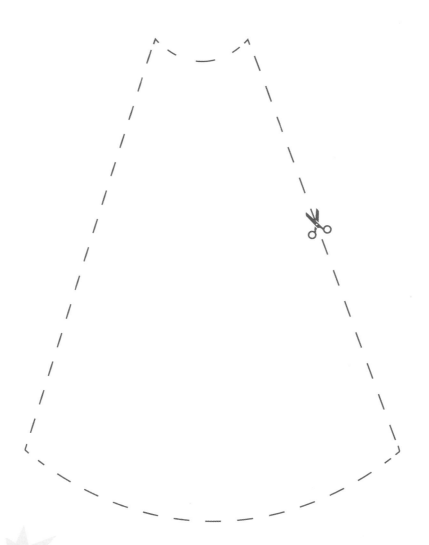

YOUR SOURCE OF
ENERGY

Wild unicorns don't need to eat much because their horn is like a solar panel that soaks up sunlight in the day and woos moonbeams at night. They don't get hungry like humans do, which makes them lucky, because they don't love grass and hay as much you'd think. It's bland and boring, except in the morning when the green grass and golden hay are dotted with dewdrops glistening with pure positivity (just like them). It's a light and refreshing way to start the day.

When unicorns do eat human food, they love red raspberries, green apples, orange oranges, pink grapefruits, and purple potatoes. They love to fill their bodies with crisp color and avoid lifeless, processed (mostly beige) foods and sweets spiked with so much sugar it gives them split ends (they like to keep their shiny manes shimmering).

Make a list of your favorite colorful natural foods that
make you glow from the inside out.

1
_____

2
_____

3
_____

4
_____

5
_____

6
_____

7
_____

8
_____

9
_____

10
_____

11
_____

12
_____

GET YOUR BEAUTY SLEEP

Some people think unicorns don't need to sleep, but they do. Being the fastest creatures in the universe, they get tired, especially the young ones after a long day of endless frolicking. Young or old, everyone needs their beauty sleep to look and feel their best.

Just like horses, unicorns can sleep standing up by shutting their long lashes for a midday snooze. But when unicorns are really tired, they prefer to lie down for a deep, dreamy sleep.

Where do you like to rest your hooves and horn every night? Cuddled up in the shadows of a big old tree? Perhaps snug as a bug in a cozy cave where you won't be disturbed? Or maybe you love to sleep out under the stars basking in the golden glow of the moonlight that energizes you with thoughts of your next day's adventures!

Every unicorn has their special before-bed, nightly routine that includes taking off their fuzzy slippers, giving themselves a glitter facial, brushing and flossing their teeth, and spending a few moments remembering all the good things that happened that day.

Now close your eyes and imagine you are about to go to bed. Doodle what you see—how you imagine your nightly routine will be—so that bedtime is a magical end to your magnificent day.

WILD AND FREE

Legends say that unicorns are so pure, only young women wearing white dresses and sitting under their favorite tree have the power to capture them. But why would you want to do that, especially when you adore and admire them so much?

When a unicorn catches a glimpse of your inner beauty, honesty, and authenticity, he or she will lay down beside you and remind you of how lovely relaxing in the cool shade of your favorite tree can be. But don't try to tame a wild horse (again, why would you want to?) or you may scare them away, never to return again.

Unicorns were born to take flight and dance in the sunlight. They were brilliantly built to be lightning-fast and flit by in a twinkle of an eye, so if you do believe, let them be. Let them run wild and let them run free.

STEP 1:
GATHER THESE MATERIALS TOGETHER

★ Glue ★ Wire ★ Construction paper ★ Tissue paper ★ Pens
★ Fabric ★ Glitter ★ Tape ★ String ★ Ribbon ★ Feathers
★ Scissors ★ And anything you think wings might be made of

STEP 2:
Make your own wings.

STEP 3:
Figure out how to attach them, then count down to liftoff... 5-4-3-2-1... GO!

LET YOUR HAIR DOWN

Have you ever been for a walk in the woods and found a threadlike strand of unicorn hair stuck to the end of a twig or thorn? Like every molecule making up a unicorn, their manes and tails are magical (duh). Even Hagrid in *Harry Potter* used unicorn hair to fix injuries, while Mandy in *Ella Enchanted* used it in her medicinal soup.

When you can't dye your hair a funky shade of fun, let your flight of fancy take off with pinks and purples (and every other color of the rainbow), and transform your long or short mop into lengthy, luscious unicorn locks.

HOW TO MAKE YOUR OWN UNICORN HAIR

STEP 1:
Find some rainbow-colored yarn (or any color combination you like). Tie some strands together at one end and then unravel them.

STEP 2:
Clip the colorful bundle of strands to your existing hairdo and—presto—unicorn hair extensions!

STEP 3:
Use a little comb to gently brush your multicolor mop of unicorn hair.

Always in fashion, you will be the life of the party when it looks as if you have rainbows sprouting out of the top of your head. You can even braid them if you like.

19

SWEET DRAGON DREAMS

If you have ever sipped a steaming mug of warm milk before going to bed, you are no stranger to the calming comfort of this simple, soothing drink, which can help you settle down and sleep. Although healthy humans and horses are over the moon about moon milk, practitioners of the ancient healing art of Ayurveda have been concocting batches of this plant-based drink for centuries to mend minds, bodies, and souls. Some of the ingredients have amazing properties: ashwagandha helps you relax; maca puts you in a good mood; antioxidants in acai help you think more clearly; and dragon fruit, well, it's pink!

Packed with sweetly scented spices and overflowing with oodles of as-organic-as-you-want ingredients, every creature who drinks this dreamy dragon potion drifts off into drowsy dreamland, so why wait until you see the first sliver of the big wheel of cheese surrounded by stars to put your hooves up? Let this recipe launch your taste buds into orbit and inspire you to season it to taste with your own talented twist.

INGREDIENTS

- 2 cups almond milk
- 1 teaspoon coconut oil
- 1 tablespoon pitaya/dragon fruit powder
- Dash of ground cinnamon
- Dash of ground nutmeg
- Dash of ground cardamom
- Honey or maple syrup (optional)
- 1 teaspoon acai powder (optional)
- 1 teaspoon ashwagandha powder (optional)
- 1 teaspoon maca powder (optional)
- Rose water to taste (optional)
- Dried rose petals, to garnish (optional)

INSTRUCTIONS

1. Heat the almond milk in a small saucepan over a medium heat until it starts to bubble and froth, but try not to let it boil.

2. Whisk in the other ingredients until they dissolve, also adding the optional ingredients if you wish.

3. Fill a mug for yourself and a friend, garnish the milk with dried rose petals (if using), and serve!

moon milk

FEEDBACK LOOPS

Feedback loops are not a new brand of cereal made by and for unicorns—feedback loops describe why people who believe they will always fail are likely to fail, because even if they get results they didn't expect, they continue on the same road, without making any changes to achieve the results they want.

People who believe they will always get the results they want usually do. And when they don't, they analyze the feedback they get, make changes (over and over if necessary), and never give up until they get the results they want.

Keep this simple system in mind to avoid getting too many splinters in your butt as you ride down the rainbow slide of life. BTW: Every unicorn has mastered feedback loops (that's why everything they do is magic). Will you remember to consider the influence feedback loops have on your existence from now on?

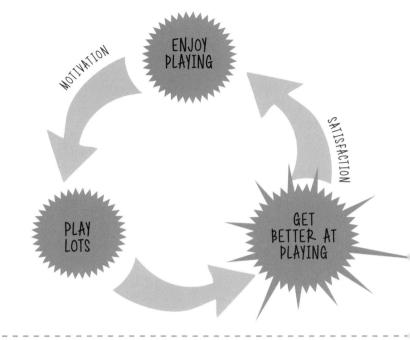

DREAMTIME

Dreams are stories we write in our sleep. What do you dream about? Whatever your favorite topics and subjects, you are a prolific writer, spinning anywhere from three to six scenarios every night.

What do unicorns dream about? Just like dogs chasing imaginary cats and cats chasing imaginary mice, you will see unicorns' hooves galloping, their tails twisting and twirling, and their ears flicking from side to side as they imagine what their dream world sounds like.

When unicorns fall into serene slumbers, they dream about running through mountain meadows in a light breeze, foraging for fragrant flowers and fresh fruit they can eat straight from the tree, and splashing in the waves and collecting sand-filled seashells at the beach. When they dream of disagreements with their friends or family, they never wake up mad; they find a solution and make up before the sun rises.

Wherever your sleepy sightseeing adventures take you, expect to meet a unicorn.

Most of us forget 95 percent of our dreams, but that doesn't mean you have to. Decorate a new notebook and call it your dream diary or journal. Before you fall asleep tonight, tell yourself you will remember your dreams, and then write them down every morning. If you can't remember them at first, don't worry. It takes practice. You will train your brain to wake up and write.

THE COLORS OF YOU

Unicorns come in all shapes and sizes, from pure white, shiny silver, and brilliant gold to sky-blue, apple-red, royal purple, chocolate-brown, and jet black. The same goes for the twinkle in their eyes, which shine with a magic so magnificent you sense you are connected on an invisible level where everyone and everything is one.

You and all unicorns came from the same stuff, and there is no such thing as being separate from this stuff that's in everyone and everything. Regardless of your history or ancestry, if you are reading this, you belong to the unicorn bloodline and are always welcome in their tribe, as they are surely welcome in yours.

Mythologists believe that if you touch a pure white unicorn you will be happy for eternity, though every unicorn and person—regardless of color or creed—is capable of connecting and celebrating the enchanting supernatural experience that comes from knowing who you really are and where you really come from.

MY FAVORITE COLORS

What are your favorite colors?
Create your own color wheel
and then color the unicorn the
colors you imagine it to be.
This will help you summon
him or her into your life.

PLAY WITH YOUR FAMILY

Just as a young grasshopper hops from leaf to twig to blade of grass and back, from the moment a baby unicorn hatches, it wants to play. Full of innocence and inexperience, unicorn parents are eager to teach them how to run as fast as the rainbow-colored rays of light that brighten the sky, and how and where their favorite foods are hiding, so they can take care of themselves one day.

Unicorn parents forget that there are things they just can't teach their cheerful colts and feisty fillies. Parents of playful unicorns don't always know how to handle their excitement and energy, so be patient with them; they weren't given a manual on how to raise a bright trailblazer like you.

They will do and say things they don't mean and make mistakes, but try to remember: they were young once too. So, if you haven't been in touch recently, make some time for your family—it's always great to reconnect in a low-key, relaxing way. No matter how old you are, everyone needs reminders to play and have fun.

Finish this list of fun things you can do with your family:

- Go for a walk
- Put on some music
- Watch a movie together
- Bake some cookies
-
-
-
-
-
-
-
-
-

FROLIC IN THE FOREST

Do you like to hug trees or lay in the grass and look up at the sky?
How about blazing trails on a hike or bouncing around on a mountain bike?
The ancient Japanese practice of *shinrin-yoku* (known as "forest bathing" to
the rest of us) encourages seekers of soothing serenity and majestic magic
to venture outside and soak up some inspiring ions in the hope of finding a
mythical creature, a spritely nature spirit, or forest elf to play with.

If you do go wandering in the wild woods yonder, take some fresh,
homemade breadcrumbs with you so you can find your way back to
homely headquarters (and feed the unicorns along the way with the
tasting menu that the birds don't get to first).

Go outside and look around. What do you see?

_____

_____

What's beautiful?

_____

_____

_____

Now look again. What is not so beautiful to you, but may be to someone else?

_____

_____

_____

Where is your favorite place in nature?

_____

_____

_____

_____

_____

_____

_____

SUMMON YOUR STRIPES

On the African continent, monochrome zebras reign supreme as the coolest of the equines. No one knows whether these wild horses who rock the last letter of the alphabet are black with white stripes or white with black stripes.

Your long-lost cousins are metaphors for the two-sided nature of reality. No matter how many minds you blow with your cultured charm and charisma, you will always have positive and negative thoughts and feelings flowing through your veins.

Zebras also have night vision, so when the dark side sweet-talks you into doing things you shouldn't do (and your unicorn wings are nowhere to be found), summon your inner zebra, show off your stripes, and zigzag like zebras do, so you can outrun the lions who think you make a pretty yummy lunch.

COLOR THIS FAMILY OF ZEBRAS
IN BRIGHT, RAINBOW SHADES

SPRINKLE SUGAR

Ogre, goblin, gremlin, human, unicorn, werewolf, or troll, everyone seems to like sugar way more than salt. Is it any wonder why? How do you feel when someone says "thank you" because of something you did or said?

You may have noticed by now that you can often get what you want much easier if you are kind and considerate, rather than if you are rude and obnoxious. Everyone wants to be happy, but struggles to see life through a unicorn's eyes. Why make it harder on everyone, including yourself?

Unicorns are symbols of pure, positive happiness, representing all the fine qualities we strive to personify and embody (which means most people want to be just like them). Act as if you always have a choice as to how you respond or react to someone or a situation, because you do!

For one day, do an experiment. Imagine you are carrying around a bowl of sugar in one hand and a saltshaker in the other. In every conversation you have, think to yourself: What does this person want more—salt or sugar?

Draw a bowl of sugar and a shaker of salt, and answer these questions...

SUGAR

SALT

Who did you talk to?

Did they want sugar or salt?

What did you give them?

Why?

What did you learn?

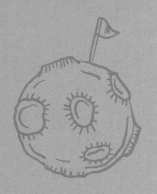

INTERDIMENSIONAL TRAVEL

How many dimensions do you think exist in ever-expanding space and time?
No one knows for sure—not even radical rocket scientists who study
astronomy and quantum physics.

Humbly hiding in the safety of a straw-filled stable is no place for a horned horse with a knack for expressing itself with flair and flamboyance. If you've ever wanted to pop into and out of other dimensions where unicorns are more abundant than stars, what are you waiting for?

Adults spend an enormous amount of time, money, and energy on classes and workshops learning how to see the world through a child's eyes. Most would never admit it, but they want to find their inner unicorns too. So get yourself a return ticket and go unicorn-ing in another dimension before you grow up too much!

37

Continued

First thing in the morning, before you even open your eyes, take a few deep breaths and try not to think about anything. This is the hard part, but it's how your imagination will take off and soar like the birds. Gently flex your muscles and then loosen them, one by one. Now pretend you are floating in space. You can go anywhere and do anything. Where will you go and what will you do?

When you get back to this dimension, record your discoveries below:

Where I went
_____
_____
_____
_____
_____

What I saw
_____
_____
_____
_____

What I did
_____
_____
_____
_____
_____

THE GOLDEN RULES

You may have heard of golden rule number 1: "Do unto others as you would have others do unto you," which means to treat others the way you want to be treated. Unicorns can't imagine not following this rule, so why doesn't everyone else? People say they want to live a more magical life, but what are they doing about it?

NUMBER 1

"DO UNTO OTHERS AS YOU WOULD HAVE OTHERS DO UNTO YOU"

NUMBER 2

"HE OR SHE WHO MAKES THE GOLD MAKES THE RULES"

Maybe because golden rule number 2— "He or she who makes the gold makes the rules"—is more important to most people than treating others how they would like to be treated. What does golden rule number 2 mean? It means we do the things people with money ask or tell us to do.

With hearts and horns of gold, unicorns great and small keep both golden rules in mind, which ensures they succeed in any field they find themselves in.

Do you follow either of these golden rules?

_____

_____

_____

Which one(s)?

_____

_____

_____

_____

Why or why not?

_____

_____

_____

_____

Do a social experiment. For one day, ask everyone you talk to if they've heard of the golden rules. With their permission, capture their (and your) thoughts in your phone as a record of your experiment. One week or month or year later, remember to ask the same people if they think or act differently based on your original conversation. Do you?

MAGIC IS REAL

Many people deny that magic exists, and ignore it whenever they see it, because if magic were real, it would mean there's more to life than they realize. If they can't see something with their own eyes or touch something with their own hands, then how can it be real?

Unfortunately for unicorns (and every other creature who has the power to pop into and out of physical existence), when people live in denial and disbelief, it's harder for them to wake up to the love and light that's twinkling quietly on the inside. This is why it seems like the majority of people are robot ostriches hiding their heads in the sand.

Deep down, you know magic is real. Whenever you think of someone and they text you, or when you just know something before it happens—these are examples of magic. Ordinary people call this intuition or coincidence, but you know the truth.

WIZARD'S BREW

YOU WILL NEED

- Glass jar
- Vinegar
- Food coloring
- Glitter (optional, but not really)
- Tray with sides
- Dish soap
- Baking soda

INSTRUCTIONS

1. Fill the jar halfway up with vinegar and add a few drops of food coloring and a sprinkle of glitter.
2. Put the jar on the tray and stir in a little dish soap.
3. Next, scoop up a big teaspoon of baking soda, stir it in, and step back! Once the brew has simmered down, add a few more drops of food coloring, baking soda, and vinegar.

SPEAK FROM YOUR HEART

What language do you speak? Did you know you also have a language based on how you express your love for your brother(s) and sister(s), (grand) parent(s), boyfriend/girlfriend, best friend, acquaintance, coach, or mentor?

If your primary love language is...

QUALITY TIME

You love undivided attention, and nothing makes you feel a connection with someone like eye contact, phone in the pocket, and TV off. You feel most loved when you relate to someone face-to-face and exchange undivided, uninterrupted, free-from-distraction attention. A lack of proper attention (along with flaky people) drives you up the wall.

PHYSICAL TOUCH

You like to touch and be touched, and show you care with hugs, pats on the back, and high fives. Being physically close to other people is important to you, and physical abuse is unforgivable. Touch is the form of communication that comes most naturally to you, and it sometimes seems as if you can't live without it.

WORDS OF AFFIRMATION

Words speak louder than actions to you, "I love you" melts your heart like a hot knife in cold butter, and you are at your best when giving and receiving praise. But when people insult you, you turn to ice and couldn't melt if they had a blow-dryer blowing full blast. Thankfully, you are unstoppable when your tank is filled with encouraging words.

ACTS OF SERVICE

When someone helps you with your work or your chores (or when you help someone with theirs), the bond you cement is stronger than steel. The actions that follow "Let me do that for you" make you so invincible not even kryptonite can stop you. Laziness and broken promises drain your energy, but selfless service makes your heart sing.

GIVING & RECEIVING GIFTS

You aren't materialistic. You soak up energy that proves people have made an effort to do something special for you, like make you a birthday card or give you a handmade gift. This is also how you show other people you care about them. Missed birthdays are the worst, though symbols of love and care speak volumes in your book.

45

Continued

Everyone has at least one, so which one do you speak, listen for, and enjoy the most?

Put a check mark beside the statements that resonate with you the most and then see if there's a pattern that reveals which love language comes most naturally to you.

- ☐ I like one-on-one time with people
- ☐ I like when someone helps me do something
- ☐ I like when people give me gifts
- ☐ I like when someone puts their arm around me
- ☐ I like spending time with my friends and family
- ☐ I like when people say they love me or I did a good job
- ☐ I like sending or receiving thoughtful texts
- ☐ I like giving and receiving hugs
- ☐ I like talking or doing things together
- ☐ I like when people touch me
- ☐ I like to tell people how much I love them
- ☐ I like when people give me compliments
- ☐ I like it when people listen to me when I speak
- ☐ I like giving gifts to my friends and family
- ☐ I like when people ask me about my feelings
- ☐ I like when someone close to me touches me
- ☐ I like when people help me with my chores
- ☐ I like when people give me special gifts
- ☐ I like having someone's undivided attention
- ☐ I like going places with people I care about
- ☐ I like to give people hugs and high fives
- ☐ I like when people don't interrupt me
- ☐ I like when people remember my birthday
- ☐ I like surprise gifts from my friends or family
- ☐ I like to make eye contact when I talk to someone
- ☐ I like giving compliments to people

However you connect with people, don't disregard other communication styles. Everyone you know speaks one of these love languages most of the time. Just like learning a few words in another language guarantees you have a better experience when you travel overseas, learning to speak other love languages will make every relationship better.

P.S.
GOOD RELATIONSHIPS
ARE THE SECRET TO
HAPPINESS.

AIM FOR YOUR NORTH STAR

You are stardust and dandelion fluff, so don't let anyone tame you if that's not what you want. Wild at heart, you know life is a game and games are for playing. You are like a character in a play or the main character in your own movie.

There are millions of people in the world who always knew what they wanted to do and who they wanted to be when they grew up. All they did was find the unicorn inside of them and ride it until they got where they wanted to go. You may know where you want to go and what you want to do, or you may need more time.

Once you decide, simply saddle up (or ride bareback) and don't stop until you get there. Your horn is like a compass that will help point the way to your North Star: the wish, itch, desire, or dream that makes you feel happier than anything else in the world. Find it and follow it forever.

Draw a picture of how your life will be when you reach your North Star.

What can you do to remind yourself every morning and night of your aim?

_____

_____

_____

_____

_____

_____

_____

_____

PIE IN THE SKY

Sweet-tempered and well-liked, unicorns are not aggressive, which means they have few (if any) enemies. Although poachers are on the lookout for an elusive trophy or two to hang on the wall above their fireplace, you have nothing to worry about, you dashingly dignified creature of ether with the gift of lift. If ever you're in danger, flap those well-built wings and fly!

Unicorns easily defend themselves (or any other innocent creature they consider kin) with an effortless beam of celestial light that protects anyone in their aura from any threat, real or imagined.

Revered for their strength, unicorns are the best bouncers at the cosmic nightclub-slash-bakery called Pie in the Sky that's open 24/7. Everyone is welcome (including poachers, who are required to pass through security and check in their weapons) because unicorns don't discriminate.

What is your favorite kind of pie?

_____

_____

_____

Think of everyone you would like to share your pie with, then cut it into pieces and write everyone's name on theirs. Don't forget to give a piece to someone you don't think deserves one.

_____

_____

_____

_____

_____

_____

_____

_____

WHY?
BECAUSE EVERYONE DESERVES PIE!

FOLLOW YOUR
BLISS

Being a unicorn is about following your bliss, no matter what. Embracing the values and virtues that unicorns represent while prancing around the world with a pure heart, doing good deeds, and celebrating delicious delight is what being alive is all about.

Being a unicorn-powered prince or princess is not about acting like you are something you're not and chasing things that don't fill your heart and soul with joy, just because someone else thinks you should.

You will get all the attention and admiration you could ever want when you don't need it. What's the best way to not need it? Live like you already have it. One of a unicorn's favorite words is irony: when the opposite of what you expect to happen happens. The joke is that it almost always happens! Watch the goodies flow into your life like a waterfall when you start pretending like you don't need them.

1 List everything you are good at. Can you sing, dance, write, or draw? Do you like to help people or build things? Spend 30 minutes on this a few times over the coming week to get all your ideas out.

2 The more you believe you can do something—and/or that help is available—the more likely you are to take action when you get inspired. Stay connected to what makes you feel alive and you will step into the infinite unlimited universe where unicorns are everywhere. Where does your inner power come from? Describe it below.

_____
_____
_____
_____
_____
_____
_____

_____
_____
_____
_____
_____
_____
_____
_____
_____
_____
_____
_____

3 The more you play and practice the things that bring you joy, the more you will believe in bliss. You will see opportunities to help other people, make the world a better place, and put a smile on someone's face.

THERE IS NO LIMIT TO YOUR UNICORN POWERS.

HARNESS YOUR HORSEPOWER

In the 18th century, we began using the word "horsepower" to compare steam engines to our nearest and dearest. Did you know your body generates electricity, even when you're sitting still? The days of hand-cranking radios and flashlights and plugging your cell phone into a charger are numbered.

Every step you take and every move you make is kinetic energy that, via your shoes, clothes, keyboards, and backpacks, can potentially power your electronic devices, collectively run the generator at the gym, and light up dance floors whenever you bounce up and down to the beat.

Speaking of burning off excess energy, it's likely only a matter of time before we figure out a way to channel a few watts of excess energy into burning fat. How's that for a diet? Hold on for dear life; the future is bright (even if it seems like tech is presently running on pony power).

Metabolism is another word for all the chemical reactions in your body that keep you alive. The higher and more revved-up it is, the better your body and mind look and feel. Keeping your fine form in tip-top shape is what makes you such a prize-winning mare or stallion, regardless of how out-of-this-world you are.

Use this checklist to start keeping track of your metabolism hacks, so you'll be fully charged and able to power up instantly, no matter where you are or what you're doing. Feel free to create and come up with your own, and stick it on your wall.

Date	To Do	Done (Gold Star)
	Sweat	
	Drink water	
	Lift weights	
	Eat breakfast	
	Sleep soundly	
	Eat veggies	
	Laugh	

FLOW LIKE WATER

Yielding to cosmic traffic when you're popping up here and there delighting unsuspecting mortals with your priceless presence can be tricky, especially when everyone is moving so fast chasing this and that on their way to who-knows-where.

It's easy to forget how to let go and let life flow. What do you do when a stone gets stuck in your hoof, or a burr lodges itself in your soft fur coat? Flowing like water softens the sharp edges of things around us, allowing the complicated, convoluted, and complex stuff to evaporate into thin air. By going with the flow, we know which way to go at every fork in the road, so we never have to swim upstream.

Your majestic horn can only grow longer and stronger with time, so let the wisdom of your sharp antenna guide and direct your thoughts, feelings, and actions toward the people and projects that you most wish to enrich with your custom brand of spellbinding, watery wizardry.

Draw what you would look like if you were water.

BELIEVE IN YOURSELF

Even if you don't believe in humans (serves them right for not believing in you), they believe that they exist (so, for all intents and purposes, they pretty much do). But all unicorns must be patient with them—they have limited psychic abilities and sometimes forget how to play and have fun.

That's why you exist: to bring good fortune to all who believe in you. You bring joy to those who suffer and find those who are lost. Just having the confidence they may actually find you and be whisked away to a misty mountaintop meadow is enough to help a lost soul hear what their heart has been softly saying all along.

Precious and pure, let's tell it like it is: you are the ultimate antidepressant. It's why every kid on earth smiles when they see a soft, plush stuffed toy sitting on a shelf that looks just like you: the essence and embodiment of pure joy.

BELIEVE IN YOURSELF
AND OTHERS WILL TOO

58

Hold this page up in front of your face like a mirror and see how bright and beautiful your smile is, and how it lights up your life and everyone's day when they see it.

GO
OUTSIDE

How much screen time is too much? No one knows. When you start getting worried that your eyes are going to turn into squares, remind yourself of how awesome blowing off steam in the fresh air is.

It's hard being perfect all the time. Try finding ways to get your kicks in old-fashioned ways, so you don't go getting excited and start kicking your hind legs and breaking something you don't want to break (lower your risk by going to the backyard or the park).

Unicorns don't live or work or play in houses. They live, work, and play outside. So, if you want to be more like a unicorn, act like a unicorn. Who cares what your bike looks like with rainbow ribbons growing out of the handlebars, or how dashing your knee-high socks make you look?

50 WAYS TO PLAY OUTSIDE

1. Plant a vegetable garden
2. Go horseback riding :)
3. Have a picnic
4. Sidewalk chalk
5. Fly a drone
6. Take a hike
7. Watch the sunrise or sunset
8. Have a garage sale
9. Go miniature golfing
10. Tube down a river
11. Go to a farmers' market
12. Ride your bike
13. Jump on a trampoline
14. Make mud pies
15. Have a water fight
16. Go swimming
17. Go for a walk
18. Blow bubbles
19. Skip stones
20. Climb a tree
21. Make a compost bin
22. Go fishing
23. Fall asleep in a hammock
24. Pick berries
25. Find a waterfall

26. Fly a kite
27. Roller-skate
28. Hula Hoop
29. Read under a tree
30. Eat homemade popsicles
31. Wash a car
32. Search for bugs
33. Pick flowers
34. Find shapes in clouds
35. Paint rocks
36. Do cartwheels
37. Build a fort
38. Walk barefoot in the grass
39. Eat ice cream
40. Clean up your neighborhood
41. Go to the lake or beach
42. Watch for shooting stars
43. Play with a ball
44. Play Frisbee
45. Let a helium balloon go
46. Wave at people in passing vehicles
47. Watch grass grow
48. Sell lemonade
49. Mow the lawn
50. Build a sandcastle

HOW TO MOVE MOUNTAINS

Motivation is more than being interested in something and getting excited about it. What really counts is when you dig in your spurs, tug on your reins, and put one hoof in front of the other until you get where you want to go.

There are two types of motivation: extrinsic and intrinsic. Extrinsic motivation comes from external influence, like what your friends, family, boss, or teacher want you to do. Intrinsic motivation is driven by your inner desire to do something, like how much pleasure you get from learning something new or practicing something you love.

Turns out the more intrinsically motivated you are to become the best winged horse you can be, the easier it is to stay motivated, overcome challenges, leap over *Homo sapiens*, and reach your goals waiting for you in the star system at the end of the double-rainbow galaxy.

Write your number 1 goal for the next 12 months on the line below.

MY NUMBER 1 GOAL:

_____

_____

_____

_____

Then list as many intrinsic and extrinsic motivators you can
think of that will inspire you to stay on your path.

MY EXTRINSIC MOTIVATORS	MY INTRINSIC MOTIVATORS
•	•
•	•
•	•
•	•
•	•
•	•
•	•
•	•

THE COLORS OF THE
RAINBOW

Rainbows and unicorns are like hot chocolate and marshmallows, shooting stars and first dates, or peanut butter and jelly: they were made for each other. The rainbow flag celebrating the diversity of the LGBTQ+ community was created by American artist Gilbert Baker in 1978 and has changed the way we see the world.

In the LGBTQ+ community, rainbows symbolize fabulous self-acceptance, and no matter who or where you are, unicorns symbolize every playful and colorful expression of masculinity, femininity, fluidity, and everything in between.

Although our fine furry friends tend toward their feminine side, it's no surprise that everyone adores these mythical equines. Unicorns are exceptional, emblematic metaphors for what it means to be both magical and mortal, male and female, grand and humble, just as everyone in the world is at their core... regardless of shape, size, stance, or style.

COLOR IN THIS PICTURE

GROW
YOUR BRAIN

Your brain is made up of billions of tiny nerve cells called neurons, and these neurons are connected by a network of over a trillion tiny branches of chemical signals called neurotransmitters, which are responsible for everything your body can do.

Your brain loves to work as efficiently as possible, so when you repeat a thought or experience a feeling over and over again, the signal becomes stronger, which makes it easier for you to repeat the thought or feeling in the future.

Just like when you lift weights your muscles grow, when you practice or learn something your brain grows, changes, and gets stronger—just like a muscle. Scientists used to believe that our brains stopped growing, but we now know our brains keep growing bigger and heavier, just like a unicorn's powerful leg muscles that propel them off the ground and through the air.

Continued

STEP 1: AWARENESS

Everyone has a little voice inside of them, but it usually criticizes and doubts whether or not you can do something. It says things like:

- I'm not good enough
- I will probably fail
- I can't do this
- I shouldn't have to try so hard
- If I'm not naturally good at this, I should just quit

Give your voice a name. It will remind you that it's just a habit of thought—it's not you!
I will call my inner hater

_____

What makes your doubter speak up?

_____

_____

What does your inner voice say when you want to try something new or learn a new skill?

_____

_____

What does your inner voice say when you think about changing something about yourself?

_____

_____

What does your inner voice say when someone criticizes you?

_____

_____

What does your inner voice say when you get a different result than you hoped for?

_____

_____

When someone makes a mistake... Do you judge them? Criticize them?

_____

_____

What does your inner voice say when you're under pressure or have a deadline?

_____

_____

What does your inner voice say when you are feeling lazy and procrastinating?

_____

_____

What does your inner voice say when you are arguing with someone?

_____

_____

What does your inner voice say about what other people think about you?

_____

_____

_____

_____

Continued

STEP 2: PERSPECTIVE

You can't always change what happens, but you always have a choice when it comes to how you see a situation and how you respond and react (and how you tell yourself the story of what's happening or just happened).

The next time you catch your inner critic in the act, thinking thoughts that make you feel the opposite of how you want to feel, ask yourself: What's happening here?

How else could I look at this situation? What's good about this? What might the other person be thinking, feeling, seeing, or perceiving?

Here are some examples of how a shift in your thinking can quickly change your brain:

When you think: What if I'm not good enough? What if I fail?
Change it to: Everyone starts from scratch and has to learn how to do something they don't know how to do. People fail all the time.

When you think: It's not my fault.
Change it to: If I don't accept responsibility for my part, I am powerless.

When you think:
If I was naturally good at this,
it wouldn't be so hard. I suck.
Change it to: If it's hard, it means I just have
to put in more effort and practice every day.
It will be awesome when I can do it
with my eyes closed.

When you think: If I don't try,
I can't fail.
Change it to: If I don't try,
I have already failed.

Now look back at how your inner hater likes to mess with you, and rewrite a NEW thought for each careless criticism and debilitating doubt.

My negative thought

My positive thought

Continued

STEP 3: ACTION

Congratulations! You've begun to change how you think. This next step is important too, because the best way to grow your brain is to put what you learn into action and apply it to real life.

What did you learn from this experience?

_____

_____

What can you do differently the next time your inner voice wants to derail your progress?

_____

_____

What would help you achieve a goal you haven't yet taken steps toward achieving?

_____

_____

What do you need to learn or practice?

_____

_____

What are the steps you will take?

_____

_____

_____

Action step	
When will I do it?	
What will I need?	
Goal/outcome	

Action step	
When will I do it?	
What will I need?	
Goal/outcome	

Action step	
When will I do it?	
What will I need?	
Goal/outcome	

Action step	
When will I do it?	
What will I need?	
Goal/outcome	

YOU HAVE PERMISSION

Who decides what you can and can't do? You? Just like our inner critic who never shuts up... wait a minute... how did they ever get their nonexistent hands on a megaphone, and how in the world did they figure out how it works?

The older you get, the more you will see your habits, hopes, and fears only mean something if you decide they do. You don't need special permission from anyone in your life. As long as you aren't hurting yourself or anyone else, you are allowed to live your life any way you choose. Do you think unicorns ever worry about getting permission from someone who doesn't care about them? Never!

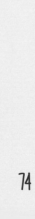

Write yourself a permission slip, adding every inspiring and empowering affirmation that gives you goose bumps and butterflies when you think / write / read about it.

Dear _____

I promise to _____
_____

I want to remember that _____
_____

I forgive myself for _____
_____

I want you to know that _____
_____

I'm so happy that _____
_____

I love knowing _____
_____

You now have my permission to _____
_____

You also have my permission to _____
_____

(Sign your name) _____
(Date) _____

FORGIVE THE BULLIES

Unicorn philosophers faced with poisoning themselves with regret and thoughts of revenge seek a bird's-eye view instead and ask themselves: What would my great-great-great grand-unicorn do?

The next time someone does something you don't like, instead of thinking how you will never let them off the hook, imagine the one person you admire most in the world. How would this person react to the situation? Would they fight or hit back? Would they stomp off and pout? Would they devise devilishly devious ways of getting back at them?

Forgiveness doesn't mean you forget, ignore, pardon, or place blame somewhere else. Forgiveness is about accepting the fact you were in the wrong place at the wrong time, and are still holding onto anger and resentment that only hurts you. Not being able to forgive others (or yourself) will keep you going in the opposite direction from where you want to be. Keep going that way, and you will never find your inner unicorn.

"The weak can
never forgive.
Forgiveness
is the attribute
of the strong."

Mahatma Gandhi

WHAT WOULD A UNICORN DO?

When we don't know which way to point our horn, we procrastinate and worry ourselves into a tornado of a tizzy, wondering why life seems so difficult, even though we can fart rainbows and fly at the same time.

Making a decision can be hard, but lack of perspective is the only issue, so put your problem through its paces and think it through from different points of view. Knowing your strengths, what would your mom say? Knowing your weaknesses, what would a lion (our worst enemy) say? What would you do if you were immortal (like we are rumored to be) and will live forever? What would you do if today was your last day?

There is no such thing as a perfect decision, though by tilting your head and looking at your dream or dilemma differently, you will feel optimistic and make a courageous yet calculated choice based on the bigger picture.

Option 1:

_____

Option 2:

_____

What's the best that could happen?

_____

_____

What's the worst that could happen?

_____

_____

What strengths support me?

_____

_____

What weaknesses require strengthening?

_____

_____

I have decided to

_____

_____

_____

_____

YOUR MONKEY MIND

One song that should be on every
unicorn's playlist begins like this:

YOU HAVE A LITTLE VOICE INSIDE YOU.
IT DOESN'T MATTER WHO YOU THINK YOU MAY BE.
IT DOESN'T MATTER WHAT YOU THINK YOU BELIEVE.
YOU'RE NOT FREE, IF YOU DON'T KNOW ME.

The only problem is most people can't hear their little voice because
there's a monkey running amok, not only making a mess of things
(that you have to clean up in between all your other chores),
but also stressing you out with its constant chatter.

Unicorns love this lyrical reminder of how easy it is for humans to get
distracted by the monkey mayhem going on in and around them at all times,
when all it takes to make ooh-ooh-aah-aah sit still and listen for once is
quieting the mind so that we may hear what our inner unicorn is saying.
What is he or she saying? Only time and silence can tell.

1
Close your eyes and take a deep breath.

2
When your monkey gets annoyed (it will), just playfully pat him or her on the head and take a deep breath.

3
Breathe in as slowly and as deeply as you can, hold your breath for a moment, and then breathe out until there's no air left in your lungs.

4
Do this every morning or night for five minutes and your monkey will clean up its room, curl up on the couch, and sleep through the night so you can do the work you were born to do.

MIRROR MIRROR

MIRROR MIRROR ON THE WALL,
WHO'S THE MOST DELIGHTFUL OF ALL?

YOU, OF COURSE!

Looking deeply into your own eyes can change your life (every dashing, debonair descendant of the three-toed desmatippus who went extinct five million years ago knows this). It may seem simple or silly, but simple and silly are how the best things in life disguise themselves. Everything you think or say is an affirmation that programs the software in your brain.

Looking into a mirror and repeating positive affirmations to yourself is one of the most effective ways of learning to love and appreciate yourself and feel safe in the world. Affirmations plant seeds of self-confidence and self-esteem that will flower into fruit.

Are you resisting something or allowing it to flow? The more you do mirror work, the quicker it will become mirror play, and the sooner you will start taking care of your precious self in a powerful way.

1. Sit or stand in front of your bathroom mirror.

2. Look into your eyes.

3. Take a deep breath and say:
I want to love you. How about it?

4. Take another deep breath
and say: I'm learning to love you.

5. Say it again, using your name
as if you're talking directly to yourself.

6. Every time you see your reflection,
repeat these affirmations, even silently.

Mirror work can trigger deep emotions. You may feel angry;
you may want to cry; you may laugh and smile and giggle at
yourself. Let yourself experience and express every feeling.
Say something kind and caring to yourself every day—whatever
words, thoughts, and feelings come to mind—and you will see
there is no limit to the love you can express and experience.

THINGS YOU CAN'T BE TAUGHT

When poet and playwright Oscar Wilde said that anything worth knowing could not be taught, perhaps he was referring to emotional intelligence: a simple, pure, basic understanding of how we are connected to everything around us.

No matter how much you study what other people have to teach, this effortless yet extraordinary awareness is something you naturally learn on your own when you have compassion and consideration for other people, places, plants, and animals.

Unicorns know this already: their intuitive instincts (intrinsically) motivate them to travel, listen, read, think, share, and invest their time and energy exploring their environment—solely to appreciate, accept, and tolerate every single way of living and being.

Soak up every minute and experience, and learn as much as you can, even about things that make you angry or scare you. Question and query everything, for knowledge is power.

Continued

Pretend you are on the International Space Station looking down at the Earth. Draw what it looks like to you and then answer these questions:

Have you ever traveled far from home?

_____

_____

Where did you go?

_____

_____

_____

Who did you meet?

_____

_____

What did you see?

_____

_____

How did you feel?

_____

_____

Would you go back?

_____

_____

Why or why not?

_____

_____

Where will you go next and why?

_____

_____

What do you hope to find or see?

_____

_____

_____

so GOOD IT'S TRUE

How do you get to splash around at the waterpark all day (every day) when most mortals are stuck at their desks working or studying and dreaming of sliding down sun-soaked, corkscrew-shaped waterslides with you?

You may long to achieve what's beyond your reach, dreaming abstract dreams and concocting far-fetched schemes, just as you should be. There is more to life than meets the eye. Wants, wishes, hopes, and desires sprout in the invisible world and spring forth into tangible being (though not without intention, action, and patience).

Your goals gleefully glistening beyond gates guarding distant galaxies glitter with gold for a reason. Great things want you, too. Among the fastest creatures in all of creation, unicorns are born with enough enthusiasm and affection to pursue their passions with purpose and hatch any egg they lay. Unicorns make their own luck, so never believe in limits when it comes to making magical miracles happen.

START HERE

YOU ARE BEAUTIFUL

We all have biases based on our beliefs and background that determine what we consider beautiful. Stop supposing for a split-second and ask yourself: What is beautiful to me? Even though fancy filters on photos want you to believe the most popular social-media mavens are perfectly perfect, it's far from true and you know it.

Rocking your curves, scars, and warts makes you remarkable. So few of us have the courage, confidence, bravery, and backbone to be ourselves, that we aren't used to it. Loving your love handles and taking pride in your pimples will beam your beauty into the world in an uncommon yet extraordinary way.

Vain vampires only survive by sucking the blood out of the people who blindly follow them. Don't get bitten! You have heaps of glitter to sprinkle across the cosmos with your tailor-made, custom-built good looks. Book covers are inspired by the contents (which can't help but shine through), and it's the same with you.

HOW TO BE BEAUTIFUL

understanding
HONESTY PASSION
INDEPENDENCE
sense of humor
ORIGINALITY
kindness
LOYALTY
DECISIVENESS intelligence
confidence

TREASURE MAP

When you seem to be repelling (instead of attracting) everything you want, and feel more like a rhinoceros with a picture of a unicorn taped to your wall reminding you to "never give up on your dreams," it's easy to get frustrated and stop believing in yourself.

Never fear, my dear. Your head, heart, and horn are in the right place. Don't give up and rip up the pictures and posters adorning your special space. Think of all the images, objects, doodads, thingamajigs, and whatchamacallits you collect as reminders of your desires and proof you are on the right path.

Everything you can do to evoke the thoughts, feelings, beliefs, and habits that align you with your crushes and cravings will act like clues and guide you to your buried treasure.

Collect a stack of magazines you like to read, some scissors, a glue stick, and a piece of poster board or cardboard, and give yourself some time and space to start snipping, gluing, organizing, and designing your dream life. Cut out words and images and anything that excites you or gives you butterflies. Think of your collage as a treasure map, reminding you of the personal and professional treasures you seek, and hang it somewhere you will see it every day, like on your wall, on the ceiling above your bed, or on the back of your bedroom door. This is so much fun, you may want to make one every year.

SWEET SOLITUDE

Do you have a hard time being by yourself?
Unicorns love spending time alone and stocking up
on this invisible ingredient in the secret sauce recipe
to their award-winning charm.

Don't be fooled. A two-week vacation is never enough
(it takes that long just to untangle the knots in your
mane and catch your busy-bee, bucking-bronco breath).
Curl up in a cabin in the woods to write your book, and
surrender to the seclusion of your peaceful pottery or
sewing studio, because the fewer the distractions, the
more productive and creative you will be.

Studies show that folks who enjoy their own company are
less stressed and less depressed than those who don't,
but you don't need to go and get yourself shipwrecked on
a deserted island—just start enjoying your own company
more. Turn off your phone, go for a walk, and let your mind
wander, because it was made to run free.

Set a timer on your phone for an hour or two, and see how long you can go without speaking to, or interacting with, another person.

I'M NOT TALKING TO YOU!

AWAY WITH ANXIETY

Even though it looks as though unicorns are always happy, they too have their down days. No one and nothing is perfect. Just like you, they get nervous about going to a new place, being interviewed for a job, or being the center of attention.

When they feel restless and have a hard time concentrating or falling asleep, they know the antidote to anxiety is a candlelit bubble bath or batch of chocolate chip cookies. You may not always be able to shoo the butterflies from your stomach, but the well-meaning, beautiful bugs trying to alert you to danger won't get so excited when they know what's coming: some soothing self-care.

With time and practice, you too can learn the ways of wise unicorns whose wisdom lies in getting enough sleep, in remembering to breathe, in eating colorful, nutritious, delicious fruits and vegetables, and minimizing toxic thoughts, people, and places. Unicorns don't go nuts: they stash them away to share with squirrels in the middle of winter when it's cold out.

In one column, write a list of what makes you feel anxious and uneasy. In the second column, write what you plan to do when the butterflies and squirrels get together and plan a coup d'état.

THIS MAKES ME FEEL
ANXIOUS AND UNEASY

MY HAPPY PLANS

THE GIFT
OF GIVING

If you have an abundance of love, time, money, or energy to give (and you aren't already shining your rainbow light into the world), what are you waiting for? If you feel like you can't keep your inner unicorn in, your job is to help others remember who they really are.

Unicorns of all ages and abilities beam with the knowledge they are benevolently blessed to be bursting with bliss. They have plenty to give and never consider the possibility of giving too much. P.S. The happiest people are those who share their love, time, money, and energy with others.

While everyone has a unicorn inside of them, most people are saddled with so much responsibility they have forgotten how to throw off their harness and run free. So if you see a unicorn trapped inside someone you love that wants to come out but can't, you know what to do.

People who haven't found their inner unicorn sometimes only do thoughtful or generous things because they expect to get something in return, but this always backfires. When your heart is in the right place, the backward law comes into effect and will always give you way more than you give.

Make a list of ten ways you can easily help others find their inner unicorn:

1 _____

2 _____

3 _____

4 _____

5 _____

6 _____

7 _____

8 _____

9 _____

10 _____

TWIST AND
SHOUT

Ever wonder what life would be like if you could do anything? What if there were no limits to what you could taste, touch, do, say, feel, and experience? No doubt movies, magazines, and popular blogs on every possible topic inspire you with the notion that anything and everything is possible. But what if it was?

When you eventually get a warm whiff or tantalizing taste of sweet success, heavenly happiness, or fleeting fulfillment, enjoy it in the moment, ride the wave, and let it crash on the shore when it wants to (trying to hold sand in a fist never works). Why do you think unicorns are happy most of the time?

Unicorns know joy and sorrow come and go—these feelings are enduring and ephemeral evidence of the humble beating heart and powdered sugar-coated soul of existence. They dance in the dreamy, dualistic delight of transient time and space, an experiential escapade that has existed longer than suns have shined on solar systems a gazillion light-years away.

Pretend you own a nightclub for unicorns. Create a colorful dance floor, keeping in mind your customers' footloose and fancy-free, four-legged dance moves.

HOW TO BE SAD

Unicorns aren't positive all the time. Even these perpetually positive, perky ponies have days when they feel like they stepped in their own you-know-what. What makes these magnificent mammals so impressive is they know how to turn terrible into terrific.

Depression seems like a four-letter word to a unicorn, for they know that having a purpose in life (reminding people to chase rainbows, in their case) feels much better than feeling sad. When you focus on something more important than how much your life sucks, most bad days go and sulk in the corner where they belong.

So when the next stop on the cotton candy express spells negative, numb, gloomy, and glum, find a creative outlet that will express your melancholy misery in a crazy and colorful way.

WAGE A POWDER-PAINT WAR

Choose your space. This activity will get messy, so ask for permission if necessary. Gather some friends and tell everyone to wear white. Divide yourselves into teams or just give everyone their favorite paint color, and let the games begin!

Conserve your powder-paint ammo in squeeze bottles or paper or plastic cups, or make a color grenade by filling pantyhose or socks. They will poof on contact and can be used until they run out.

TIP:
WEAR SUNGLASSES OR SWIM
OR SKI GOGGLES TO PROTECT
YOUR EYES.

HORSE & CLOWN AROUND

Playfully pirouetting around the planet as they please, unicorns are known the multiverse over for their positive position on all things good-natured. Naturally gifted with an optimistic outlook, these welcome exceptions to the rules of the animal kingdom, known for their prominent forehead protrusions, represent the polar opposite of a defeatist daydreamer distressed by doomsday.

Trust your stars are always aligned in divine design and are guiding you with good-luck charms, omens, and signs. Listen to your heart when it says to let your inner clown out, as this is often the best umbrella to open when the dark clouds of life roll in and pesky problems start raining on your parade, beauty pageant, or afternoon tea party.

When you forget what life is for (like everyone does), awaken your inner unicorn from his or her sleepy slumber and tenderly remind yourself of who you really are, so you may forever find the freedom you need to amuse yourself with good-humored horseplay.

Pretend you own a beauty salon and a unicorn needs your help to get them ready for a birthday party where they are (obviously) the guest of honor. Put your cosmetic touch to the test.

ACT AS IF

Do you ever imagine living a different life? We all might as well be wearing horsehead masks, because we are always acting. So why not try on a better version of yourself for size? How does your best self think? How do they feel? How do they behave? How do they walk? How do they talk? How do they spend money? How and what do they eat?

When you want to change something about yourself, decide what you want your new behavior, thought, or belief to be, and then, just as if you were creating a character in a movie, describe everything you can about their habits, actions, thoughts, and feelings.

Now, for the next 24 hours, act as if you are living life as your new self. It feels weird at first, but only because you are so used to doing, thinking, feeling, saying, and believing that you are a certain way (which you don't have to anymore).

Continued

MY BODY

I will act as if my body is:

_____

The words I use to describe my body are:

_____

_____

MY HOME

I will act as if my home is:

_____

The words I use to describe my home are:

_____

_____

MY JOB

I will act as if my job is:

_____

The words I use to describe my job are:

_____

_____

MY RELATIONSHIPS

I will act as if my relationships are:

_____

_____

The words I use to describe my relationships are:

_____

_____

_____

MY PERSONALITY

I will act as if I am:

_____

_____

_____

The words I use to describe myself are:

_____

_____

_____

_____

_____

_____

_____

_____

_____

_____

YOUR SUPERSONIC EARS

Author and professor Leo Buscaglia (known as Dr. Love) believed that "listening is love in action." You have two ears and one mouth, so listening requires that you do twice as much of it than talking. Who always listens to you? Who never seems to be listening?

Do you consider yourself a good listener? Do you truly care about other people and getting to know them (and what makes them tick) better?

Unicorns the universe over have mastered the admirable art and subtle science of listening. How else would they be some of the wisest beings in existence?

Focus 100 percent on people when they speak to you and you will find that the more you listen, the more people will share their deepest hopes, fears, dreams, and ideas with you. What a way to connect and make people believe there is more to life than meets the ears!

The next three conversations you have, remember to listen, and then afterward fill this page with all the things you learned about the other person—or yourself—that you would never have known unless you truly listened.

1. What did you learn about _____ (name) or yourself?

_____

_____

_____

_____

2. What did you learn about _____ (name) or yourself?

_____

_____

_____

_____

3. What did you learn about _____ (name) or yourself?

_____

_____

_____

_____

KEEP CALM
AND
RIDE A UNICORN

No one can rain on your day when you sparkle from within. The ticklish twinkle in your eye and suave spring in your step are enough to weather any weather. Storms will come and go, so it's up to you to paint your own rainbow. If anyone can, it's you.

Never let someone turn off your light or shut the door on your dreams. Unicorns don't lose sleep over the opinions of donkeys who have had their tails pinned down.

"Uni" means "one." There is only one of you, just like there is only one Sun in our solar system. Be a unicorn in a field of horses, even when it's dark and dreary and wet and cold, either in your life or deep down in your soul. Just like the Sun, you always shine. You might just have to rise above the clouds and hold on to the saddle for dear life, but no matter how bumpy the ride gets, hold on, stay calm, and keep on going.

HOW DO YOU LIKE TO STAY CALM AND CARRY ON?

STAY CALM AND

Complete your own Stay Calm poster, based on some of these examples.

USE YOUR IMAGINATION

The most famous yellow aquatic invertebrate on television wasn't the first to utter such profound undersea (and thus overland) wisdom, though proud proclamations from a simple spoke-sponge in animated form does tend to resonate with creatives of all ages.

Cartoons, caricatures, and unicorns are so well-liked because they live like there is no limit to what is possible in the endless expanse of our collectively connected infinite imagination. They don't doubt it for a second, so neither should you.

Apart from getting the hang of sprinkling sweet sugar and warm fuzzies everywhere you go, finding your inner unicorn is about learning to let your imagination loose so your mind's eye can see what others can't. Again, creative creatures of all kinds do this on a daily basis, and they don't even know that's what they're doing.

Your imagination is constantly soaking up information like a sponge and storing it away for safekeeping. In your own words or images, scribble or sketch all the ways your imagination makes your life more magical and meaningful. Let your ideas, thoughts, and feelings flow and spill out onto the page for your mind to absorb (like a sponge) to use later.

GET BACK ON
THE UNICORN

Don't be scared of making mistakes. Whether you are dating, selling widgets, perfecting the perfect pie crust, learning to drive, learning a musical instrument, writing a book, mastering your favorite sport, coding an app, running for office, or saving the whales, until you have fallen off the horse over and over again, you won't have what it takes to come out on top.

Most people don't know what they don't know, and only through repeated effort in the face of obstacles can they learn more than they thought there was to know. Happily, the only way to learn these crucial things is not only to fall off the horse, but to get back on it—over and over again—until you learn how to keep your balance.

The more horse-powered your drive, and the higher the heavenly heights you wish to climb, the thicker the skin you will need. Get back on your horse, brush off the haters like fleas who laugh at you because you're different, and feel free to laugh at them, as they're all the same.

Play a game to see how many times you can get rejected. Make a list of everything you tried and the outcome. P.S. You will be surprised at how quickly you get a YES!

WHAT I TRIED

WHAT HAPPENED

WISH UPON A STAR

These four words sweetly sung by a green bug wearing a top hat and tails named Jiminy Cricket in the Disney movie *Pinocchio* inspire us with an enchanting message celebrating how anything is truly possible when we believe in magic.

We make a wish when we blow out the candles on our birthday cake, or toss a coin into a well, but how often do we see a shooting star? We crave to catch a glimpse of the glowing tail of a meteor as it enters the Earth's atmosphere, coveting this cosmic experience, and so, of course, we give it special meaning.

What if belief was all it took to grow a tree from a seed you planted in the sea of our galaxy? What if turning your dreams into reality was easy?
You don't need a genie to grant your wishes when you're a unicorn.

When you wish upon a star
Makes no difference who you are.
Anything your heart desires
Will come to you.

If your heart is in your dream
No request is too extreme.
When you wish upon a star
As dreamers do.

Fate is kind.
She brings to those who love
The sweet fulfillment of
Their secret longing.

Like a bolt out of the blue
Fate steps in and sees you through.
When you wish upon a star
Your dreams come true.

Leigh Harline & Ned Washington

SING YOUR SONG

Unicorns don't sing because they're happy; unicorns are happy because they
sing. How sweet and savory a sonic landscape of noise and silence can be
simultaneously. Notes and tone, rhythm and rhyme, voice and pitch
and string pluck and strum, and beats per minute, and hypnotic drones.
Pan playing his flute would agree.

How can music be described with human words? Error-prone language
cannot describe the indescribable. With or without lyrics, everyone can
channel, interpret, articulate, and express emotion via melody and harmony
in perfect pitch (or not): there are no rules to sound sculpture.
Anyone can make music, just as anyone can cook.

You don't have to play an instrument to voice your thoughts and feelings.
That's what sticks and coffee cans and vocal chords and hands and feet and boxes
and squeaky doors and computers are for. What do you have to sing or say?
What is music to your ears? Make a sound, any sound. Even if it's a neigh!

Write the song your inner unicorn
wouldn't be shy to sing in public.

YOUR SUPERPOWER

What if you saw your greatest weakness as your
greatest strength? You would only have to believe
in it long enough to take a few unsteady steps to
see proof of what you're capable of.

The only thing standing in your way is you. You have
to "believe in it" before you can "bring it." When has a
unicorn not believed in something? How dare we entertain
the thought. As babies bumbling around lovingly learning
how to walk, they don't give up one day and say:
"This walking thing is hard—it's not for me."

Unicorns know they were born to be great, so why would
us hairy humans with all our super-powerful potential
bulging and bursting at our seams not naturally feel the
same way? Because we simply don't believe we are brilliant
beyond belief. But what else is life for, if not to be the best
brave beings we can?

What is your superpower? Describe it in every detail, using every sense and skill and sip of secret sauce you can come up with, to create a supersized you with the letter "U" emblazoned on your chest.

_____

_____

_____

_____

_____

_____

_____

_____

_____

_____

_____

_____

_____

_____

_____

_____

_____

USE YOUR NIGHT VISION

What do you do when you can't see beyond the tall trees or heavenly horizons up ahead? What do you do when your crystal ball is clouded over in a dense foggy mist as gray as a dreary winter's day and tomorrow seems eons away?

Competing with the crazy competition clamoring for the world's attention on social media or at school or work is emotionally and physically draining (not to mention spirit-dampening). So what if millions of people have nothing to say, but keep saying it? What do you have to say? What are you being called to do?

No one can ever say it or sing it or sew it or write it or play it or build it or bake it quite like you. So precious are your unique unicornian projects that any other bold bucking bronco in his or her right mind can't imagine not pursuing their passions, no matter how dark or obscure the path ahead. Remember: at night, a candle is brighter than the Sun.

What would your inner unicorn do or say if it knew you had unwrapped its gift to you (a pair of night-vision goggles that can see through anything), but never used them? Imagine you have picked them up and are looking through them now. What do you see ahead of you?

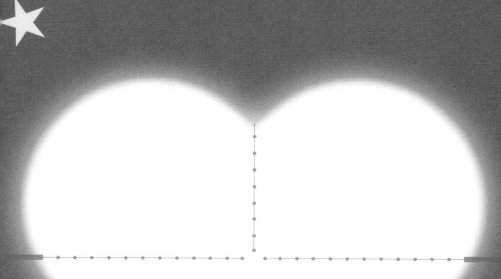

YOUR LEARNING STYLE

Everyone has different learning styles, strengths, and strategies. Some unicorns find it easier to respond to input and information via their eyes: like looking at photos or watching a movie in their mind. Other unicorns relate to their environment via their ears: they can hear things others can't, and enjoy listening to lovebirds sing. The other type of lion-tailed, goat-bearded, deer-footed, fairy-tale beast this book is designed to help you find is able to understand and connect with the world through his or her body or tactile feelings.

The popular philosophy of learning styles was originally intended to help counselors and coaches convince their clients that it was possible to change their lives and achieve their goals. Play with these ideas to find out how you can study better and learn new things faster.

Pretend a unicorn has come to you for help (you never know). Let them get comfortable on your couch or in your courtyard, and then interview them using the questions below to find out how they tune into the world around them. Your goal is to help them become more self-aware, so they can happily fire you and get on with their legendary lives.

1. What seems to be the trouble?

_____

_____

2. A friend wants to hang out with you. Would you rather:
   ☐ go to the movies   ☐ listen to music   ☐ bake a cake

3. Do you like to: ☐ draw   ☐ sing   ☐ run

Now make up a few of your own questions, close your eyes, and pretend your uni-client is answering you. Write his or her responses in the space provided.

_____

_____

_____

_____

_____

Add up the responses and, based on your findings, advise your uni-client to study in ways they enjoy, and minimize struggling through ways they don't.

FAR FROM HOME

Have you ever felt at "home" anywhere else than where you usually live? Not only is the Earth a big place (duh) with numberless nooks and countless crannies, your imagination is deeper than a bottomless wishing well where you can experience anything that tickles your fancy with your five or more goddess-given super senses.

Many people—including breeders who take care of precious ponies both tall and small—feel like home is where the heart is, just as sentimental bumper stickers and wall hangings like to remind us.

No matter how far-flung our experimental adventures take us galavanting across the globe or into the inner shrines of our soul, no unicorn, human, angel, or other blessed being is ever far from their heart's home when they are close to their nearest and dearest in body or in spirit, for few things matter more than being with like-minded and kind-hearted kin, however they are related (or not), and wherever they are in the world.

When was the last time you spent a significant time away from home?
Was it a week? A month? A year?

Where did you go?

_____

_____

What did you learn about yourself?

_____

_____

Were you excited and/or scared?

_____

_____

How did you celebrate or cope with the new experience?

_____

_____

_____

If you've never been away from home, where do you imagine you would like to go?

_____

_____

NATURE SPIRITS

Fact or fiction, the elemental realm makes up most of what we don't see when we are out and about. Simply and unpretentiously vibrating at other frequencies, whether you believe in ethereal entities or not is up to you. By now, surely you know the only limits you experience are those you have placed on yourself.

Back in the good old days, the line between the mythical world and this one was paper-thin (unicorns still lovingly reminisce about it). It was so much easier to believe in things we couldn't easily see or comprehend, because, well, they were everywhere and everyone believed in them!

It's not so easy nowadays, which is why we keep the legends alive and protect the armies of fairies, the battalions of brownies, the swarms of sprites, the packs of pixies, and the legions of leprechauns keeping the balance. What would we do without them? The next time you pick a flower, ask your guardian nature spirit for permission first. That's what unicorns do.

Pick and press a few of your favorite flowers
here for safekeeping.

YOU CAN FLY

Relatively earthbound, unicorns can't easily flit
around without a care as much as we'd like them to.
Though according to legend, if a unicorn and a Pegasus
(a flying horse) mate, their babies can fly!

Whether you believe it or not (and whether your parents know it or not),
they too have a unicorn inside of them. Maybe one of them even has
phenomenal Pegasus genes. Okay, who do you think is more likely
to have been blessed with such a rare gift?

Chances are you've got the same genetic material somewhere in
your DNA that only needs to come to the surface. Every critter and
creature is always evolving, so why not learn how to take flight?
Trampolines and flying lessons are a good start, as are dreams and virtual
reality simulations. There is no limit to how high you can fly.

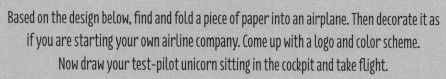

Based on the design below, find and fold a piece of paper into an airplane. Then decorate it as if you are starting your own airline company. Come up with a logo and color scheme. Now draw your test-pilot unicorn sitting in the cockpit and take flight.

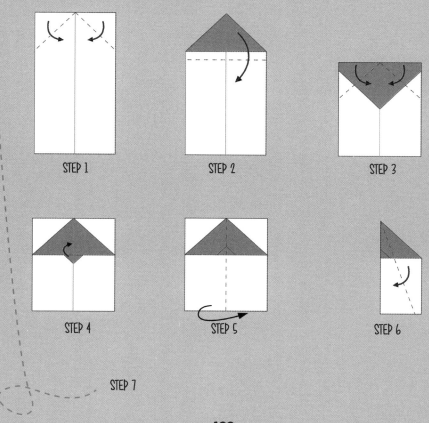

STEP 1

STEP 2

STEP 3

STEP 4

STEP 5

STEP 6

STEP 7

CREATE YOUR OWN LANGUAGE

Why are we/they called unicorns and not unihorns? In the British Isles, where the English language took shape, the accented, voiceless, velar fricative sound "h" came out of people's mouths more like the scraping "ch" sound, which is how "horn" became "corn."

Did you ever make up your own language that only your brother or sister or friends knew how to speak? With approximately 6,500 languages spoken in the world, there's surely room for one more.

While it may never catch on like Mandarin Chinese (which is spoken by 1.2 billion people), why let that stop you? However we communicate—with words, books, body language, sounds, songs, or games—sending and receiving new information in creative ways is what makes life interesting.

Make a list of your eight favorite words. How can you communicate the essence of each one in a new way?

GET CREATIVE!

1

....

2

....

3

....

4

....

5

....

6

....

7

....

8

....

THE WAY YOU LOOK AT THINGS

Ever laid on your back, tilted your head back, and looked at the world from upside-down, imagining what your life would be like back-to-front and inside-out? If most modern philosophers and physicists' theories are even close to correct, perception is reality.

Did you know humans can see 7 million colors? We see the world in combinations of three colors: red, green, and blue, while most animals see only in yellow and blue (how boring). Some birds, fish, and reptiles have it good: they can see four colors, including ultraviolet and infrared light.

Now imagine unicorns have the combined capability not only to see the world like those gifted four-color creatures, but also the capacity to see something like 10 million colors? Think rainbows are awesome from a human perspective? Imagine how they must look to a unicorn!

"Look deep into nature and you will understand everything better."

Albert Einstein

HOW TO SOLVE PROBLEMS

First of all, no matter what the problem is, stick with it until it's not a problem anymore. Scores of strategies and plenty of procedures exist to expedite your quest, though no tactic matters if you give up before you piece together the perplexing puzzle and find your way out of the mind-boggling maze you got lost in. It doesn't matter how slow you go, as long as you don't stop.

Second, common sense says we can't solve a problem by thinking, feeling, or acting in the same way that we were thinking, feeling, or acting when we created or caused the problem in the first place. While this is a bit of a brain boggle, it's also a blessing in disguise, encouraging us to use our noodle and come up with oodles of solutions. Then all we have to do is throw these pieces of potentially perfect pasta at the wall and see what sticks.

HERE ARE THE FIVE STEPS TO SOLVE ANY PROBLEM:

1
Get perspective—how would other people solve this problem?

2
Define the cause (not the symptoms) of the problem.

3
Brainstorm all possible solutions, alternatives, and outcomes.

4
Weigh each alternative against your values—what is important to me?

5
Make a decision, take action, and make changes as needed.

FROM THE
HORSE'S MOUTH

Hearing something "straight from the horse's mouth" means the information came from a trusted, reliable source. It's an idiom that is believed to have originated at the racetrack where a gambler got a tip from the horse itself before placing a bet.

Critical thinking is crucial when everyone has an opinion and there is so much fake news stuck in traffic along the Infobahn superhighway screwing things up. When learning, studying, reading, thinking, writing, wondering, and communicating, it's critical to get your information not only from a source you trust, but also one that resonates with your highly tuned intuition.

Unicorns don't believe everything they see, read, or hear from just any old horse in the race. There's a reason some horses always win and some never place (it has nothing to do with the jockeys, weather, lucky numbers, or new horseshoes). Don't believe the hype (not even all the flowery phraseology in this book).

Unicorns are
awesome.
I'm awesome.
Therefore,
I'm a unicorn!

TAKE YOUR TIME

Slow learner or late bloomer—however you see yourself or you imagine other people see you, try to ignore their judgment. Just like a unicorn learning to walk, fly, or summon the courage to go and find a new pasture to play in, memorizing, studying, and acquiring a new skill takes time. Be patient with yourself and your progress, however fast or slow you go.

There are no rules or timelines to success, or to getting married, or to building a business, or to starting a family. The only lifestyle rules that apply to you are those you choose to adopt and follow. There will always be people brighter or duller than you; others who know more or less than you; and those who have more or less than you.

Comparing yourself to others is the quickest way to get (and stay) depressed. Deep down, you—and every other unicorn establishing themselves in the world— have everything you need to accomplish anything you want (or not). If you need to, pretend you are a slug-slow sloth who is free to sleep all day and/or go at your own pace.

SUCCESS

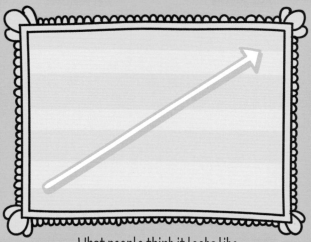

What people think it looks like

What it really looks like

FIND YOUR TRIBE

Unicorns not only find deep delight in sweet solitude, they also love making new friends who expand their horizons. Their curiosity is met with open arms, warm smiles, and holy horsehair brushes when they venture out of the safety of the stable and seek to understand how others can live so differently, yet still somehow manage to enjoy life.

While friends are worth more than gold to a unicorn, quality trumps quantity every magical moment. Celebrating friendship and fellowship while weathering the ups and downs with your clan is the greatest joy in life, besides being able to eat candy all day long and never get cavities, or being able to fart rainbows that don't make people run away screaming.

When you find your tribe, you won't need candy to make yourself happy, and when you fart, everyone will laugh along with you, not at you.

Design your perfect companion, so you will know them when you see them.

WHAT THEY LOOK LIKE

THEIR FAVORITE FOODS

EXTRA-SPECIAL POWERS

FAVORITE THINGS TO DO

ARTISTIC SCIENCE

Long ago, the Greeks and Romans believed that nine muses, all personified as women, were the source of every ounce of creative inspiration. Each presided over an artistic or scientific discipline of the day, such as music, poetry, history, or astronomy, and were celebrated for bestowing their innovative ideas and inventive insights on the many mere mortals who seemed to enjoy the enlightening experiences.

These days, all you have to do is listen for the wistful whisper of inspiration flowing from the lips of your own inner muse, and have the courage to do its bold or humble bidding. Whether you are a sensitive artist or a serious scientist, every precious pony on Earth can harness infinite inspiration and make magical miracles happen. Which muse are you?

"OIL AND WATER"

YOU WILL NEED
- Watercolor paint
- Plates or plastic containers
- Cooking oil
- Watercolor paper
- Tray with edges (this can get messy!)
- Eyedropper

INSTRUCTIONS

1. Mix up some paint in a couple of plates or containers.
2. Pour some cooking oil into another plate or container.
3. Put your watercolor paper in the tray.
4. Drop by drop, let the watercolors and oil decorate your paper.
5. Stop before your fine-art science project turns brown!
6. Carefully move your masterpiece away from your workspace to dry overnight.
7. What interested you the most? How the various colors combined into different designs, or how the oil, water, and paper interacted with each other?

YOU-NIQUE

Each and every human has been given at least one of these nine types of intelligence, along with the mission to cultivate and share it with the world. Just like our universe may be part of a multiverse—comprised of many universes that contain every particle of matter in existence—our brains are multidimensional too.

We have all been given special talents, which, when combined with our other abilities, give us the power to do great things. We are as unique as the patterns in our retinas and fingertips, and everyone has different strengths. The more you know about yours, the better chance you have of finding your inner unicorn.

VERBAL INTELLIGENCE

People with verbal-linguistic intelligence have a way with words and are great storytellers. If you like to read, write, and edit what you (or others) write, try learning how to speak unicorn (or the language of a country or region of the world that speaks to you). The world is a big place just waiting to be explored by you.

2

MATHEMATICAL INTELLIGENCE

With mathematical reasoning ability, you have an uncommon knack for applying systematical thought processes to your problems and coming to logical conclusions. You are a natural at separating true from false and you love making sense of things. You want to believe unicorns are real—you just need to prove it somehow!

NATURALISTIC INTELLIGENCE

Do you naturally gravitate toward plants, trees, flowers, and animals? Maybe you want to be a biologist or botanist, grow a garden, or raise animals (unicorns love it when you brush them). Perhaps you are happiest when you're outdoors hiking, surfing, climbing mile-high mountains, or spelunking with vampire bats.

Continued

VISUAL INTELLIGENCE

You have the gift of navigation and can effortlessly sense distances, differences, and spaces between you and other objects. You notice details, visualize outcomes, and make decisions based on your observations. Judging how far and fast you gotta go to catch that unicorn over there is a piece of cake for you.

SOCIAL INTELLIGENCE

Interpersonal intelligence gives you the ability to talk to anyone (which will come in handy when you have to introduce yourself and your friends to your new friend—you know, the one with the horn sticking out of his or her head). Your ability to understand other people is a faculty you employ with finesse. Some people call it emotional intelligence.

PHYSICAL INTELLIGENCE

Able to make your body do what you want it to do, you have a sharp sense of timing when you've been endowed with bodily-kinesthetic intelligence. You likely enjoy playing sports, dancing, and making stuff—like a new saddle or set of horseshoes for your pet unicorn. Remember: your physique is your best friend.

MUSICAL INTELLIGENCE

Musical, rhythmic, and harmonic intelligence has blessed you with the power and sensitivity to sense the nuances of music: rhythm, rhyme, tone, timbre, meter, melody, and pitch. You can (or could easily) play an instrument or three, and write and compose your own songs. Just so you know, unicorns love music.

INTROSPECTIVE INTELLIGENCE

The ability to understand yourself is a slow dance and a mosh pit. Sensitivity and self-reflection are profoundly powerful tools in a toolbox. You seek to solve the mysteries of the mind, and are able to see things in yourself that others can't see in themselves, which ensures you will never be bored on your quest to find your inner unicorn.

9

SPIRITUAL INTELLIGENCE

When all else fails (which will never happen when you are tapped into your talents), existential awareness is how you're going to find (or become) your own inner unicorn. With such power, unicorns will be eating whatever they eat right out of your hand. Fear will disappear, evil will evaporate, and butterflies will fall asleep on your shoulder.

Which one (or more) of these great gifts were you given? And how will you live up to the fortunate challenge that has been bestowed upon you?

INVINCIBLE INVISIBILITY

Ever wanted to be invisible? Everyone knows unicorns can bend time and space to their wishes and thus alter the way they perceive reality. One of their favorite ways to do this is to render themselves (and anyone in their sacred circle of trust) invisible.

This is why it's so hard for scientists to study them: Unicorns can see these studious scholars coming a mile away. And poof! They've vanished into thin air. Though the lucky among us—whether we commune with our inner unicorn every night before we fall asleep, or search far and wide for the elusive majestic manifestations of our inner magic (s)elves in the mountains at the ends of the earth—can only see what we believe.

Following your intuition makes you naturally invincible. So, if you ever feel like disappearing for a while, know that the only entities that will be able to see the "real" you are those who share your pure heart and sweet soul.

Round up some fun friends and play a game of hide-and-seek. When you hide, imagine with all your heart and soul that you can render yourself invisible. Really believe it.

Now think how you would act differently—today or tomorrow—if you really had the power to be invisible:

What would you do first?

_____

_____

_____

What next?

_____

_____

_____

Why do you want to be invisible?

_____

_____

_____

How would you use your invisibility cloak to help people?

_____

_____

_____

_____

THE LEGEND OF 10,000 HOURS

Knowing something back-to-front, inside-out, and upside-down makes you a Jedi Knight. Put in the time, attention, energy, and focus studying and mastering a single subject, skill, project, or passion and the world will bow at your humble feet.

Even though unicorns all look the same, they aren't. What can you do that no other unicorn can? Developing your skill or side project to the point of mastery requires commitment, and saving your (or anyone else's) soul in service of, and in dedication to, your deepest desire requires a minimum of 10,000 hours (no unicorn gets famous overnight).

Invest your time and energy wisely and you will reap the rewards. In the meantime, tossing pennies into wishing wells waiting for your prince or princess to arrive perched atop Pegasus can't hurt either.

HOW WILL YOU GET TO 10,000 HOURS?

10,000 HOURS ÷ [ ]

HOURS PER DAY

= [ ]   = [ ]   = [ ]

WEEKS   MONTHS   YEARS

Based on your calculations, how long will it take you to reach your 10,000-hour mark?

[ ]

What will inspire and remind you of your commitment?

_____

_____

_____

YOUR PIECE OF PIE

No matter how fine, feathered, furry, or fantastic you are, not everyone is going to appreciate how much time you put into your precious appearance, shower you with praise wherever you go, or ensure everything you touch turns to gold.

As a rule of hoof, one-third of creatures (whatever species they may be) are going to love you no matter what you do, while one-third will never see shining eyeball-to-eyeball with you, zigging when you zag and zagging when you zig every chance they get.

But it gets better! The remaining one-third of people you bounce by in your day-to-day comings and goings aren't even going to notice you, let alone acknowledge your existence. Everyone is so delightfully different and can only see what they believe. So what? Knowing this helps you focus your attention on who deserves it the most.

Just as someone or something is your "cup of tea," fill one slice of pie with descriptions of the types of people, places, or things that like you the way you are. Then fill in another slice with the attitudes or perspectives that don't tickle your fancy. Lastly, see if you can come up with a few personality traits or ways people choose to live that you've never noticed or thought much about before. See? You do it too!

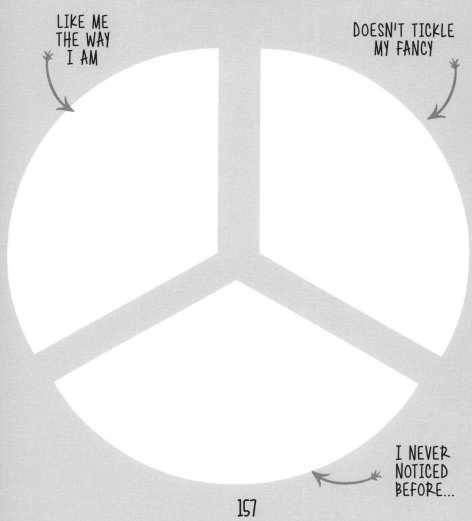

LIKE ME
THE WAY
I AM

DOESN'T TICKLE
MY FANCY

I NEVER
NOTICED
BEFORE...

FACE YOUR
FEARS

Fear is just an emotion, like happiness, sadness, or joy, and it can come and go as quickly as a bolt of lightning. In every perfect, precious moment, unicorn-conjurers like you can respond to the heebie-jeebies in countless ways. The only problem is, you are conditioned to respond in the same frightening way every time it pops out of the closet and says BOO!

Try looking at life through the opalescent eyes of a unicorn and you will see no end to how elegantly love and laughter can protect you from foreboding terror in front of your face. Instead of cowering in the corner when you get the creeps, try laughing in fear's face the next time it leaps out of nowhere and tries to scare you.

It takes practice, but living in a ceaseless state of the shivers is no fun. This four-letter word doesn't exist in a unicorn's vocabulary, so why should it exist in yours?

Write or draw something that scares you. Find something about it you can laugh at, or ways you can morph it into a joke, silly cartoon, or circus act. Feel free to play with it and edit, erase, rewrite, or redraw it to your heart's content, morphing something that scares you into something that makes you laugh.

PULL YOUR WEIGHT

Existence on any plane is filled with stuff (both tangible and not) that we all have to drag around. Luckily, you were built not only to brave any element, but also to carry the heavy load that sometimes comes with being so awesome. When people see how capable and creative you are, they see you as a leader.

With leadership comes a sense of duty. People trust and believe in you and your superpowers even more than they already did. Your inner unicorn can't help but come out and shine its (and your) light on everyone lucky enough to get close to you.

Of course, you have a choice as to the role you play and the load you tote around with you. We all prioritize what is most important to us, and make time for the people and projects that inspire us, please us, and satisfy our sense of purpose. What weight (importance or value) do you give the nouns in your life?

Cut some images from a magazine and paste them on each side of the scale based on what you tend to value or place more importance on in your life.

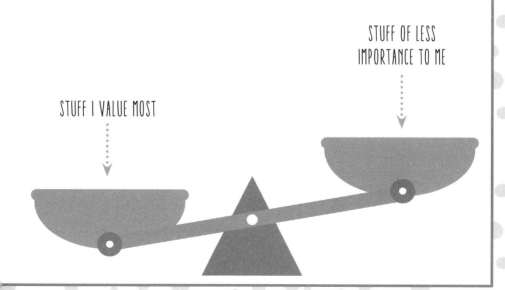

STUFF OF LESS
IMPORTANCE TO ME

STUFF I VALUE MOST

THE SECRET TO
HAPPINESS

Everyone has problems and sometimes stuff stops working. And when we solve our problems and fix or replace our stuff, new problems pop up and the cycle continues with relationships, pet projects, toys, and anything else we value.

The secret to happiness is knowing that people, ideas, and things grow and die, expand and contract, turn on and shut themselves off, run circles around us and then sleep soundly for hours, work and then don't. Everything and everyone is holding on for dear life on the corkscrew roller coaster of fragile moods and delicate emotions in the endless ocean of turbulent time. Remember that patience with ourselves and with others—along with kindness and compassion—will always lead down the pebbled path to a deep sense of inner peace that lets life be as it is, and things just as they are.

Pretend you have been invited to spend a week on the International Space Station.
Close your eyes and imagine you are looking out of a window and down on the Earth.

How do your hurdles and hiccups and worries and warts look now?

_____

_____

_____

How much do they matter?

_____

_____

_____

Do they even matter?

_____

_____

DOODLE HOW THEY LOOK
FROM SPACE, KEEPING
SIZE, PERSPECTIVE, AND
PROPORTION IN MIND.

EXPLORE THE UNIVERSE

From Ernest Shackleton and Bessie Coleman to Amelia Earhart and Sacagawea, mortals have been trotting around the globe for centuries in search of new lands, creatures, foods, and ideas (at least that's how most seekers of strange and state-of-the-art discoveries justify their exploits). What they were really after was adventure.

Beneath the surface of the seas or their souls was a hunger and thirst for understanding, knowledge, and novelty (not to mention riches). Buried and sunken treasure and the most exotic of spices and flavors drove travelers and voyagers to brave the elements near and far in search of something new.

Unicorns are natural explorers, so with all your present and potential powers to be and do and have anything in alignment with your highest purpose and for the good of all involved—and knowing the world is yours—where will you go and what will you do?

Go on a scavenger hunt. See if you can find these things, and then take a photo or keep the items in a special box:

☐ A flower you could wear in your hair
☐ A dried bird's nest
☐ A heart-shaped rock

Dream up some unusual objects or unique artifacts a unicorn would love to study, play with, or keep.

_____
_____
_____
_____
_____
_____
_____
_____
_____

UNDER THE SEA

Known as the unicorn of the sea, narwhals are toothed whales with big ivory tusks (actually a tooth) growing through their upper lip and poking out of their heads. They live in the Arctic in the icy cold oceans and rivers around Greenland, Canada, and Russia. They may or not may know they have a few distant cousins (like rhinoceroses... and you, of course) roaming around up on solid land.

Narwhals' tusks are like magic wands, spiral-shaped conduits that channel the spiritual energy suffusing and surrounding everything—antennae that easily pick up signals from their friends and family and give them a priceless polar perspective.

If you love oceans, seas, lakes, and streams, may you find the peace and tranquility you seek by soaking up the love of your soul pod that regards your sensitivity as a gift, and who will dance and sing and play with you always.

MAKE A NARWHAL TUSK

INSTRUCTIONS

1. Cut out a pyramid shape of felt.

2. Curl it into a cone, glue the edges, and let dry.

3. Stuff your tusk with cotton balls.

4. Poke them down with a pen.

5. Glue the end of string or ribbon to the top.

6. Spiral it down to the bottom and glue it in place.

7. Let dry, then cut off the extra.

8. Glue on a piece of pearlescent ribbon or paper to make a chin strap.

9. Decorate your narwhal tusk.

YOU WILL NEED

- Scissors
- Felt
- Glue gun
- Cotton balls
- Pen
- String or ribbon
- Pearlescent ribbon or paper
- Decorations (such as glitter or sequins)

AS SIMPLE AS A SANDWICH

What do you believe is possible? Do you ever think: "I can't have a sandwich"? No, you just go to the fridge, make it, and eat it. If you need mayonnaise or mustard, and don't have it, you go to the store and get some. Proud purveyors of pessimism will say dreams don't come true, but they were never let in on the secret creed that all unicorns heed: life can be as simple as a sandwich.

To unicorns, everything is a sandwich! That's why they read, study, listen, explore, and experiment so much; they get a kick out of expanding their horizons. When they see a locked door they either walk through it, or gather the materials they need to make a key.

In this way, you can literally program new habits of thought which lead to new habits of behavior which lead to new habits of action. Eventually, reaching and achieving your goal seems as simple as a sandwich, so you just go and do it, and don't even think about it.

Circle your favorite sandwich ingredients and then draw your completed masterpiece in the space provided, remembering how easy it is to make a sandwich out of anything.

HIGHTAIL IT

Silly humans—even a motorcycle called "The Unicorn" built by a big car company can only go 70 miles per hour. Sadly, their normally innovative imaginations weren't able to leave the lackluster pasture and see what blowing off some excess energy is really like.

Being so swiftly supersonic, unicorns naturally love to race. Light, limber, nimble, and quick, they can leap and hop and bounce from here to there without a care, and when determined to win a race they can turn on the afterburners and leave everyone in the dust wondering what happened, faster than rainbows appear and disappear.

Trying to get a troll out from under his bridge, a grinch out of his cozy cave, or a swamp monster to shed his seaweed and join in the fun is futile, which is why birds and butterflies are a unicorn's favorite competitors in a playful trip to the finish line at the end of a rainbow. How fast can you run? What animal do you often compare yourself to?

Color in this beautiful butterfly so it would be easy to spot as you race it to the finish line at the end of a rainbow.

TELL THE
TRUTH

You may have heard the phrase "Honesty is the best policy." In Personal and Professional Development 101 offered at Unicorn University, this course is an entrance prerequisite. Why? Because unicorns are not only believed to wield the power of divine truth, but also have the ability to "pierce the heart of a liar with their horn." So watch out, truth-stretching storytellers!

Maybe it's because unicorns are so tuned in to the unseen world behind the veil. Or maybe it's because they've been around the block enough times that they've earned their street-smart stripes based simply on their horse sense (more commonly known as common sense).

Whether you're at home, work, school, on the field, or in the forest, telling the truth—no matter how awkward or embarrassing or ego-deflating it can be—is always in your best interest. When you're not honest, life is a mess. But only until you confess. It's so important to build trust. Without it, relationships turn to dust.

Play Truth or Dare with your friends. With your unique unicorn lie-detecting abilities, sniffing out fibbing fabricators should be a piece of cake.

BE KIND

No one likes to be wrong, but so what? When casual conversation turns into an argument, debate, disagreement, or all-out war, we get annoyed, irritated, and frustrated. We dig in our heels and it's a fight to the finish.

Why do we waste so much precious energy trying to mentally overpower someone else? Because to be wrong would threaten our fragile egos, which only have survival-at-all-costs in mind (even at the expense of ending relationships). Luckily, unicorns know better and work to preserve the relationship at stake, rather than engaging in battles of you versus me.

Why would you want to separate yourself even more from someone you want to connect with? Why even communicate in the first place? If someone is determined to be right, let them be. Take a deep breath, shut your mouth, nod your head, and smile.

Think about a time when you were sure you were right about something, only to realize later that you were wrong. What happened?

_____

_____

_____

How did that make you feel?

_____

_____

_____

Do you like to be right? Do you like to fight? How do you think other people feel after a conversation or confrontation with you?

_____

_____

_____

Write down three things you will remember to do next time you enter a battle with someone you care about.

1. _____

_____

2. _____

_____

3. _____

_____

ESP

When we perceive "things" beyond the scope of our normal awareness which fall outside the range of common consciousness, we are simply using our sixth sense (known as "extra-special powers" to younger unicorns).

Can you see things others can't? Ever had prophetic dreams that came true? Or just knew something that turned out to be right? Maybe you're a natural: you think of someone and then they call or text you. Everyone can do it, especially if they're paying attention. You don't need to be a psychic, shaman, witch doctor, clairvoyant, or medium to see and feel things that aren't there.

ESP comes in all shapes and sizes, and there is no limit to what you can intuit and grasp when you are tapped into these sublime supernatural powers of extrasensory perception. Unicorns are naturally gifted seers, born with a highly developed psychic ability and sensitivity to the spirit world, but you already knew that.

Continued

See if you can match up the six types of ESP with their definitions, and then underneath each one describe an experience you've either had, or would like to have, with each type:

1
The ability to channel spirits

2
The ability to see the future

3
The ability to see the past

4
The ability to know things about someone
or something by touching an object

5
The ability to read another person's thoughts

6
The ability to "see" events or objects somewhere else

(Answers in the back of the book.)

ESP	DEFINITION NUMBER	MY OWN EXPERIENCE
Telepathy		
Clairvoyance		
Precognition		
Retro-cognition		
Mediumship		
Psychometry		

BE HERE
NOW

Have you ever felt like Big Bird, who once said: "How do I know I'm here?" If so, don't fret—it's easy for paranormally inclined ponies with a knack for knowing more than the average barn-bound hay muncher to drift into worn-out past histories or to chomp at the bit, drooling over divine destinies that exist only in the realm of future mysteries.

Where are you right now? Where is your attention? Reading this, you're here, now, in this moment, right? This instant. This split-second shake of your lamb's-ear, satin-soft, rainbow-colored tail is the only moment that exists. Everything happens in a wink, in the blink of an eye, in every now now now now now now now.

Of course, well-meaning mortals will argue that outside our perception of the collectively created mental construct of time, everything happens simultaneously. But, like all elegantly exquisite equines, you know the only place you can ever be is here and now. Ponder how the (in)significant space between two letters is the only thing that differentiates being "now here" from being "nowhere."

NOW HERE

EXPERIMENTAL ADVENTURES

What if you were a science experiment or a computer simulation, just a player or character in a game? What if gods or aliens or über-evolved humans were laughing their heads off peering through the most powerful microscopes ever invented, betting on the outcomes of our actions and behaviors as they playfully pull our strings?

If you didn't fall asleep in science class, you may remember the eight steps to the scientific method of conducting an experiment: Pose a question. Conduct research. Make a hypothesis. Design your experiment. Perform your experiment. Collect data. Draw conclusions. Share your findings.

Do you believe in fate? Just as life appears fluid, organic, and chaotic, we can be and believe in anything we want to be and believe in (even unicorns), so why not think like a scientist when designing your life? You learn to adapt governing dynamics' discoveries into practical principles that improve the quality of your life.

HOW CAN YOU APPLY THE SCIENTIFIC METHOD TO YOUR LIFE?

1. What question do you want answered?

2. Where can you get more information?

3. What do you guess the answer might be?

4. How will you test your hypothesis?

5. What happened in your experiment?

6. What happened the second time you tried it?

7. What did you learn?

8. Who else might be interested in your findings?

I AM 100% RESPONSIBLE

Most people (whether aware they are wranglers of their inner unicorns or not) believe they deserve special treatment from their friends, families, community, or government. This disastrously destructive belief is called entitlement.

When someone feels entitled, they morph into sad, sorrowful souls who snuggle up to suffering and seek to blame others for causing the chaos in their lives. The last thing unicorns want is to curl up and curse the world—they know they have the power to adapt to every good and bad thing that happens to them and not blame anyone for anything.

Entitled people are constantly angry, jealous, and frustrated. Obviously! No one gets what they want when they expect others to just give it to them. Instead of blaming others for your inner and outer obstacles, you listen to your inner unicorn instead, right? He or she is always whispering in your ear, reminding you of your magic mantra:

EVERYTHING I SEE IS UP TO ME!

Continued

When you feel like the butt of a big joke but you're not laughing, ask yourself:
HOW CAN I PUT A POSITIVE SPIN ON THIS?
HOW CAN THIS HELP ME?

Example:
Instead of complaining, "I got a parking ticket. Why me?"
or "I hate _____," how about thinking: "I shouldn't have
parked there," or "I will follow the rules next time,"
or "I'm happy to pay a tiny tax for being able
to enjoy this part of town."

Now it's your turn. Think of a time when instead of devolving into a disfigured demon you "owned" your part in whatever happened to you. Describe what happened, how you turned it around and flipped the issue upside-down, and walked away proudly wearing your cap of responsibility like a king or queen's crown.

SPEAK UP

Most of us (whether we have unearthed our inner unicorns or not) believe everything we say is being heard and understood, but you would be surprised at how much actually doesn't get through to the person you are trying to communicate with.

Some researchers believe that 55 percent of our communication is interpreted through body language, 38 percent via our tone of voice, and only 7 percent by virtue of the words we speak.

Examining an interaction with an equally interested person can be an enlightening experience when you see how much of your preplanned, premeditated broadcast falls through the cracks and fails to transmit the intended information and meaning. It's almost like you've been living in a fantasy land, nearly knocking you off your unicorn!

Considering the above, how do you plan to approach your conversations in the future? The more conscious you can be of how you relay the information, the better chance you have of making your inspired and innovative ideas heard.

After you have a conversation with someone, divide the first pie into three slices, based on how much of each style of communication you used:

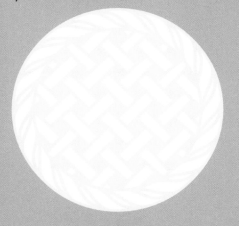

SLICE 1
Verbal language

SLICE 2
Body language

SLICE 3
Tone of voice

Now, using the three slices below, divide the second pie into three, based on how effectively you think you communicated during the conversation:

SLICE 1
We understood each other

SLICE 2
We kind of understood each other

SLICE 3
We completely misunderstood each other

AVALANCHE OF APPRECIATION

If unicorns wore clothes, this would be their ace up their sleeve. They use this simple trick to transform fear, doubt, hopelessness, and sadness into joy, love, light, and hope before they get sucked into the depths of despair, never to be seen or heard from again.

So incredibly powerful is this magic trick that it proves magic really exists. Want to know the secret to turning cynical clouds and rogue rainstorms into sweet sunshine and rapturous rainbows?

Take a look around and ask: "What's good?" When was the last time you smiled as you appreciated your fingers and toes and eyes, ears, and nose? Life would be a lot different without feet and hair and arms and legs (not to mention air and water and light and night). Did you eat today? Will you eat tomorrow? Do you have friends or family who care about you?

Who and what are you thankful for? Whether you go and tell them or keep it to yourself, let your gratitude for every breath, every drop of water, and every blink overflow like a volcano erupting with appreciation for the blessings that have been bestowed on you since the day you were born. Don't stop bubbling until you feel better.

THE SIX TYPES OF ESP AND THEIR DEFINITIONS

Telepathy — The ability to read another person's thoughts

Clairvoyance — The ability to "see" events or objects somewhere else

Precognition — The ability to see the future

Retro-cognition — The ability to see the past

Mediumship — The ability to channel spirits

Psychometry — The ability to know things about someone or something by touching an object

CREDITS

Illustrations by:

A-spring/Shutterstock; Abdilahreptil/Shutterstock; Afishka/Shutterstock; Anastasia Mazeina/Shutterstock; annadolzhenko/Shutterstock; Biara Biarovna/Shutterstock; chelovector/Shutterstock; Danielala/Shutterstock; Giuseppe_R/Shutterstock; Gorbash Varvara/Shutterstock; Honza Hruby/Shutterstock; Iliveinoctober/Shutterstock; julia_janury/Shutterstock; Kashtal/Shutterstock; Katrine Glazkova/Shutterstock; Kuzmina Aleksandra/Shutterstock; Magnia/Shutterstock; Marina Onokhina/Shutterstock; Marish/Shutterstock; Markovka/Shutterstock; MirabellePrint/Shutterstock; movaliz/Shutterstock; Nikolaeva/Shutterstock; olgasoi007/Shutterstock; Olga Yatsenko/Shutterstock; piixypeach/Shutterstock; Rachael Arnott/Shutterstock; Sandy Storm/Shutterstock; Sasha_Zabava/Shutterstock; Seda Dy/Shutterstock; Shestakova/Shutterstock; shuttersport/Shutterstock; Skaska_I/Shutterstock; SvetaZi/Shutterstock; Svetlana Kutsyn/Shutterstock; Totostarkk9456/Shutterstock; Viktoriya Pa/Shutterstock; Walnut Bird/Shutterstock; Wanchana365/Shutterstock; Zerlina/Shutterstock; and ZenStockers/Shutterstock.